# (Sage for the Wounded Soul)

(La'Shawn Janell)

# AUTOGRAPH

_____

_____

# Table of Contents

## Book 1: Ascending

- A Refreshing Unknown............................... 9
- Non-Existent Expectation .........................11
- The Middle................. ..........................14
- How Dare You ... ...................................17
- Upward and Onward................................ 20

## Book 2: Purging

- Noise Reduction ..................................23
- Surface-Level Naïveté...............................25
- A Stop or the End? ...............................27
- A Gulf of Disappointment ...........................31
- Curtain Call ....................................34
- Before You Enter ........ ...........................37

## Book 3: Reflecting

- The Strong Friend ...............................41
- Heart Safety ....................................45
- What If .....................................47
- Full Moon .......................................49
- Seasonal Shifts....................................51
- A Binding Thread ..................................53
- Toxic ..........................................55
- A Long Road of Pondering ...........................58

## Book 4: Longing

- Curious Inquiries ...............................61
- A Cautionary Plea ...............................63
- Fleeing into Peace ..............................65
- Secretly Speaking.............. .....................67
- He is Home ......................................70
- Remembering His Presence............................73
- Warm Memories ...................................75

❖ Mind Stimulation ........................................78
❖ Reminiscent Heat ..... ...............................80

## Book 5: Protecting

❖ Scar Tissue ...........................................83
❖ A Petition for Connection ...........................86
❖ The Blueprint .......................................89
❖ The Straw ...........................................92

## Book 6: Healing

❖ A Cleansing Release....................................96
❖ A Fallen Angel .........................................98
❖ Toxic Math ...........................................100
❖ A Wish to Rewind ...................................103
❖ The Final Stop .......................................108
❖ That Gear ............................................112
❖ Clear It Out ..........................................115
❖ Choosing a Melody ..................................1.17
❖ This Season ..........................................119

# Foreword

You, my friend, are able to heal, be loved and valued. Your trials and challenges are not a forever stain on your life. Not only are you able to heal, but you are **worthy** and deserve love and abundance. It is your birthright that suffering is temporary and so is this pain. Do whatever you have to, to clear it out, feel your feelings and move forward. Life does not stop at your pain points, it begins here and now. Let these words open the dark spaces. Let's shed light on what you haven't addressed and get **free**.

We have to put it out there first, though. We must identify what is plaguing us. Disease is a discomfort of the body that is trying to correct itself while discomfort is an unsettled feeling of the heart and mind, that is urging us to examine what we are avoiding. Let me tell you, Friend, the only way is through is **through**. Our feelings are signals, alarms if you will. They force us to pay attention. They stretch our limits and test our evolution. Like a plant we grow, strengthening our roots, growing out of our containers, pruning the dead parts and soaring to the sky. We are limitless, only stifled by our restricting thoughts and beliefs.

We get in our own way, thinking we are protecting ourselves by not moving forward; but that is **fear**. Fear lies to us daily. That old programming runs old tapes handed down to us. Many words and beliefs are stamped onto us through childhood yet do not actually belong to us. It's that critical voice that spawns from our upbringing but we are equipped with so much more than who came before us. We will be pioneers, too.

So, this book is for whomever feels they are stuck and may need a reminder that you can receive peace and healing, and you are not being punished when you face a setback. I promise you, I have been in your place, so my words are autobiographical while also designed for You. You'll notice the chapter names are symbolic as we step towards inner peace. It describes many phases of healing. If you are familiar with what sage does for your home and the mind, it clears, purifies and soothes. It is meant to remove negativity as we incorporate other methods to protect our dearest, most personal spaces.

As you allow your mind to explore the following subjects that may be thought-provoking and even uncomfortable, please remember that though you may be wounded, whatever you define as 'sage' in your own life will assist your troubled mind towards relief. My hope and what I'm praying for, is that my words and ponderings lead you to start a discussion with yourself, where you take a deep look at what needs to be released so that you can reach beyond your perceived limits. Allow me to walk with you during our brief time together...

# Book 1: Ascending

## A Refreshing Unknown

Today I took a step into
A path of the unknown
Untraveled roads never felt so refreshing
Like fresh snow
Or overdue rain
Wash over me and take the pain away
Hope this newness is here to stay
The left fork had bumps
Hope U-turns are okay

The Divine gave a car brakes for a reason
So we can stop for a minute
And break away from the norm
It gets boring when the lines are already engraved
So this is me taking a crayon and scribbling all over it
In Yellow
Mellow
Cool like a much-needed shade
Moistening my insides like freshly squeezed lemonade

I'm so ready for a new story
New morning glory
New asphalt
Where I don't have to halt around every corner
For the stick I'll surely trip over
Today is a new day
Took a million tomorrows to get here
But it's right on time...

I am convinced that some of us have lived many lives within this lifetime. The transformation of experience even in adulthood is massive. I'm sure I'm not the only one that struggles with change even when that's the exact thing that is needed. When we think about it, many events in our day are unknown yet we can get stuck on certain aspects and get frozen in fear.

What if we melted each layer of doubt and warmed up to the thought that the unknown does not have to be scary? What if we flipped it around to positive expectation instead of anticipating the worst? Our thoughts govern how we behave and move forward, therefore it is perfectly understandable to shy away from uncertainty. The guidance here is, even if you take a tiny step forward each day, it is better than nothing. That is progress; pat yourself on the back for doing something. Eventually, you will get closer and closer to what you are wanting to achieve and even if you experience a setback, you will at least to be able to say you tried.

## Non-existent Expectation

What is Perfection?
A glass shaped, heated and blown into
By the standards of others who are also figuring it out
Once cooled, we feel we need to stay molded
Never breaking the illusion that we could be different
Yet still beautiful...

I, though, challenge the belief
I've been thrown into the fire so much
Weakening my integrity
Yet again having the blower force air into spaces
Left sacred for the One who
Completes my puzzle without force
I jump into the fire again...
Edges frayed,
Withering,
But with faith that I have the ability to melt again
Singe the dirt and despair away
As I liquify at high temps

At my boiling point everything is clear
My resilience is here
no matter who picks me up And attempts to shape me
into their limited perception of what perfection is...

My air comes from the Creator
I sway and willingly collapse into His mold for me
Crafted by my DNA and His set of instructions
Scribed long before my star was born

I Am Perfection because I Am that I Am.
No lens of man measures up to the omniscience
That touches ALL edges, crevices and cracks

Of this earth
My birth alone came through preventative actions
So I've always been meant to blast through expectations.
And with that I forge forward.
Knowing I am my own standard.
And that is more than enough.

Societal norms and constructs will fool us into believing that being different is wrong. I do believe that notion is trending in the right direction where there is more diversity in many areas yet within ourselves, we will still compare and measure ourselves up against others, who are in their own lane. Social media isn't helpful when everyone is displaying their highlight reel and only a few show a full snapshot of how their lives are operating.

We are all susceptible to wanting to flash the bright spots and appropriately so, we keep the private things private. The illusion is that the same people we compare ourselves to, could also be struggling. When we strip away these façades, we could actually come together realizing we are all equally navigating one thing or another, and the only thing that separates us is awareness and willingness to do better and be better. Perfection doesn't exist, progress does.

## The Middle

Either our Hearts are bursting full of joy
Or bleeding furiously from the pain
It's a dichotomy of extremes
That stretch our abilities to recognize the middle

That place between here and there
Despair and care
Hearts aching from disappointment or excitement
That yearning to be free either way
To see the end as happy as it could be
Or see the end so there can be yet another new beginning

Oh, the middle is as deep as the ocean
A stillness bearing such unknowns
Brimming with childlike expectation
And tethered to the anchor of history
The weight of fears
What ifs and
F its...

The middle can be a starting point
A relief that you're not where you were
A foresight that the finish line is in reasonable vision
If not for those hidden hurdles
That clip your toe when you thought you cleared it

Those are tests...
Of your evolution
Of your progress
The learned lessons up for examination
Time being the proctor
The healer, And the dealer of the next cards
The next play is yours...

When I speak of the middle, I am referring to a place where you are floating, possibly in a state of confusion, and wondering where the land of understanding may be. The middle can be daunting because everywhere you look, you don't see a landing place in sight, yet you understand you have to keep swimming. The middle can also feel like decisions that have to be made without any other interference, and while free will is at play, so is potential regret if you make a 'wrong choice'.

The middle can be paralyzing as you analyze potential outcomes, and sometimes this can be a good problem as, most choices are favorable but taking a leap can feel huge. The middle can be a place in time where you have laid the groundwork, and you are being an observer, seeing how things play out. The middle can be a sea of uncertainty until the answers come and for others the middle can be a period of waiting, since you have given your prayers to God.

Either way, the guidance here is to define what your ground is while you are floating. Imagine there is a rock you can hold onto while the water is rushing. That rock is meant to give you a moment to breathe, catch yourself and prepare for the next waves. It it hope? Is it a sense of calm knowing it all works out in the end? Is this middle for you a time of settled emotions knowing you have lifelines in place and that you are loved and protected? Whatever that may be for you, remember that floating is okay and when we fight against the current of where we are being brought to, we may be working against what God has for us. The middle can allow you to breathe as this next blessing for you may require your full focus and attention. Lean into the middle, and rest assured that the end is in sight.

## How dare you

How dare you assume
Wish, even
That I'd remain a seed
That I'd stay small and fit into your idea of me
How silly you didn't study the science behind my growth
I poured into me
When you left me to dry
I found roots to stabilize myself
While you left me to cry

How dare you assume
Wish, even
That I'd remain a seed
Digestible
Unnoticeable
Unassuming
Choke on my branches for thinking so little of me
Sit on my leaves
Cleave to this past version of me that has long gone...

How dare you assume
Wish, even
That I'd remain a seed!!
The ignorance you breed from such a limited mind
It's damn near sad
Laughable
Unfathomable
You thought your vision of me was the absolute answer regarding
what people see
What's clear though...
Is that you've been blind
Intentional with your evil eye.
That bounces off of my ancestors protection

I'm covered.
Like a greenhouse
Fertile ground, surrounded by Divine light
Now and forever.

People can make assumptions based on their perception of us. But I've come to learn though, is how someone sees us is based on the lens they are looking through, which is very individual and can be quite limiting. The encouragement here is that some people are committed to misunderstanding you, and are therefore surprised about your progress, evolution, and ascension.

It is not for you to prove your worth to those who have a limited view of you. Your job is to shine through no matter what, and those who choose to grow with you and support you as you stretch your limits, are your people. Everyone cannot come with you, nor should be. Discernment will tell you who that is, and who that is not.

## Upward and Onward

As I rise above the clouds

I look below and see where I've come from

While looking above and marvel at where I'm going

Just under my feet are the storms that support my growth

A reminder that failure could be close

If I don't continue to aspire to my destiny

The best of me is yet to come

You would do yourself a disservice to not keep going. I know firsthand that we can look at life and wonder how many trials and challenges we can endure. We can even ask God what is that last straw, thinking that each challenge might take us out of here. Please always remember that you are Here for a purpose. Please always remember that you are loved and valued even if you did not hear it from anyone today. Each step you take can be a step closer to what you want, and even on days you feel you've hit a setback, never forget, you are supported and loved.

# Book 2: Purging

## Noise Reduction

Where my soul is traveling, this clutter cannot go
Clear out the floor so I can dance free
Move to the drum woven into my bones
I feel led to sway to the rhythm of my ancestors' chants

With this proclamation, I declare myself free of the residue
I need the noise to scurry to the corners of my mind
Hide in the dusty crevices
So I can focus
Ignite
Elevate into who I was intended to be
The stifling started early
Long before me, yet
I carry the torch of my ascended mothers
I carry them as they carry me into a vision they couldn't complete
for themselves
This is my baton I blaze through trials and make them proud

Make me proud
I refuse for these timelines to show the same movie
Over and over again on repeat
I am ready for what comes next
This hex on my elevation stops here.
The curse on my bloodline that we must endure complication
For salvation ends here

The tears we have cried
Buried in the quicksand
Keeping us from moving forward
Stops here.

Have you ever felt like there were shackles on your wrists and ankles and though your mind imagined a freer future, you physically did not know where to start? Have you felt like something was holding you back? Many times we can adopt the voices of those who came before us and now they are ingrained as limiting beliefs.

Once you realize there may be a theme to the story you have been telling yourself, the narrative that your family has created and reinforced, you have a job to do. It is not your mission fully, however if you are wanting more for yourself, you first have to declare that it is possible. Even if you think something is unreachable, you still have to speak out loud, everything that you desire. You have to speak it like it is already done. Affirming in the present, everything that is coming toward you will start to lift the veil of these limiting beliefs. I am not asking you to believe it, but I am urging you to state it, and absorb it until you do. Your brain does not know the difference, and will accept what you say as truth, so you may as well tell it something good - over and over again. Soon enough , in divine timing, what feels far away and unattainable will be in your orbit and well within your reach. Rejoice now that it will happen.

## Surface-level naiveté

All they see is skin
Not the chin
The big brown eyes
Not the smile that serves as a smokescreen
A gateway into desires
All they see is skin
A socially constructed facade of privilege
Of less stress and strife
More opportunities
And the lessened likelihood of getting shot without question

Yet...I bore
I swore never again through the pain of a needle in my back
So I could protect my son from getting stabbed in his
I cried, and placed my agony on a shelf
So I could have both hands free to smell reality
And ponder the job we were just given
I endured low iron so our son could be as strong as intended
I've earned stripes I'll never be ashamed of

What's baffling is it's mainly OUR people
Marveling at the lack of melanin
Brainwashed into thinking genuine access
The golden pathway... is gained through the perception that lighter
is better
We cracked the egg only to discover the chicken
Is singing the same song
Crowing at the sun
And running away from it at the same time
When will we truly celebrate our individual standards?
With this beat upside our heads
It's hard to figure out where to begin
Because all you see...is skin.

Colorism continues to plague us, and it makes me sad. For as far as we have come, we take several steps back into a slavery-minded mentality when we discuss and marvel at our skin colors. The more that we repeat it within our culture, the more people outside of our culture normalize these discussions, and perpetuate this fallacy that only destroys our progress.

We have to stop being a part of the problem. It's not funny, nor is it mature to continue a rating system that we cannot control nor help. It is classist and counterproductive to what we say we are about. We must dismantle the standards, knowing we are the original people full of melanin that can soak up the sun and reflect its rays back in gratitude and pride.

## A Stop or the End?

The twinkling behind me instantly
Strikes fear and annoyance simultaneously
While I'm rehearsing 'the script'

Behaviors learned for survival
Knowing it may not matter if I do the right thing
Wrong things have happened to well-meaning citizens
Tragically snatched from life to death
And I just want to make it home
Whole.
In-tact.

The fact is sad
A routine traffic stop
And I can't stop thinking about
Oscar
Philando
Sandra
I can't stop thinking about
My son in the backseat
The defeat he'd have to explain if this goes left

I take a deep breath
Ground myself
And there's a *pound* at the window
The backseat window
With my son on the other side of it
Now he's confused and scared
And I don't feel prepared to stifle the war
Instantly boiling inside of me

How exactly am I to juggle his fear and my rage?

Tap- dance out of this bullshit on society's stage where anything goes?
Where caskets and cases get closed without justice
Decorum and motherhood collide
Manners and madness reside in
The same body that wants to protect
And has to reject all militant urges not to curse this jerk out

I look Officer Over-zealous dead in his eyes
With the courtesy I know so well
While every part of me is silently screaming
WHY THE HELL WOULD YOU DO THAT
The particulars are typical
A Non-critical infraction I can own
Yet my face of stone wore the blood of my people who met their fate
With shit like this

Shakily I express my every move verbally
"I'm reaching in my purse to grab my ID"
"I'm moving slowly so that you can see"
"That I want to get out this easily and seamlessly"
"Please don't kill me"
"Please let this be a fleeting memory that doesn't stick with my baby"
"I don't need this to be breaking news"
"I don't need my loved ones flinging up my shoes in tribute of me"
"I need to see tomorrow"

I can feel my son's sorrow without locking eyes
And I realize the watery frustration was about to leak out
I'm asked for proof that my car is insured
Struggling to pull my emotions from the frozen worry
The ice in my veins attempting to cool down this pulsating fire

I require nothing but to get out of this safely
Bravely, I muster up the strength to be neutral and calm
While simultaneously saddened with flashbacks of those
Who did not survive to the next dawn

Many people know that I grew up close to law-enforcement. I had a parent that served in that capacity for over 20 years. So, I wouldn't say I had a disdain for police however, I did experience a couple of occurrences where the officer was not so nice and actively antagonizing. Never though, had I experienced a pull-over with my son in the car, and that enhanced every thought and emotion I had.

The fact that this officer startled my son put other emotions instantly into orbit. Unfortunately, I could not help but be overwhelmed by images of traffic stops gone wrong. I mention my knowledge of 'the script' because it gave me an advantage over a layperson that was not familiar with this kind of training. I had preparation that many others are not privileged to gain. Yet here I am just as scared and fearful for my life while my son is watching it play out and has his own perceptive qualities. It enrages me that I had to entertain a series of unfavorable possibilities over something so simple. Those feelings informed me that, though I have an enhanced understanding of law-enforcement based on my upbringing, in that circumstance, none of that mattered and I felt just as vulnerable and helpless as anyone else. I pray it will not always feel this way yet I have enough awareness and evidence that it may not change. All I can do is evoke a prayer of protection and hope for the best.

## A Gulf of Disappointment

I saw forever in a bottomless void
A vacuum of uncertainty
An abyss of drowning in scarcity
Yet I blindly chose to focus on the bright light in a dark storm

The warnings screamed loudly
A 5-alarm blaze
Crying for me to change course but...
I honed in on his humanity
And dammit if he didn't exploit my grace and flexibility
This almost killed me honestly

There's this intersection of getting it
And getting hit by blows you don't deserve
It's like we inherit this martyred nature that
If we endure the worst
Suffer through the fire
Pry naively around a forest of dysfunction
We somehow
Though bloodied and bludgeoned
Walk away with a trophy

This notion of making it
Getting 'there'
With this unfair takeaway that we have to suffer
With longstanding loyalty
An overaccommodating devotion
To scraps.
To an unhealed unevolved shell of a being
We accept as whole

How boldly we blast through the flags hoping this is different
What's apparent my love is we are indeed conditioned

To fight for a prize just out of our reach
We prepare for a battle that was never ours
But the projection has us dancing on a stage
Crafted on sticks
Soiled by their past experiences
Projected onto us to fix…

With this thought, I implore you to discern the difference between
Caring and carrying
Support and sacrificing
Devotion and dying inside
It's a thin line between loyalty and losing yourself
Choose your health and sanity over a shaky union
Proven to have you questioning your identity

You are whole without them
You stand tall despite their shortcomings
Your path is written and is never to be hidden in the shadow of your
doubts
Shout out to your inner child that she can rest
She is safe
And anytime those primal urges reduce you
To thinking you're not enough
Gently reply 'I am more than I ever imagined'
Ground yourself in the roots that reach down layers of generations
Here the decree of your mother's grandmothers crying "rise up my
child"
There is more for you
We didn't die for you to lie down and take this nonsense

We must know when it is our time to exit. What I can share is being a person with empathic, caring, and nurturing nature is that many times I have been hurt by understanding someone a little too much. Adding in the fact that I am a therapist wove in more threads where I felt like I had to fix situations that I did not cause. If you have been where I have, you understand that having patience is an intricate dance. Too much patience and you end up resentful. Too little patience, and you may cut someone off before fully knowing what you could have. Deciphering between those two concepts can be a confusing continuum and hidden under the overthinking and analyzing, you may have lost parts of yourself.

Love does not need to add confusion and struggle in order to declare you have done the work. 'The work' does not have to be excruciating to be successful. Somewhere along the way, many of us have misconstrued giving effort with enduring constant challenges beyond reason. That line can be difficult to tease out when you love someone and are invested. I am here to say, though, that we do not have to suffer endlessly for the supposed prize of commitment and matrimony. We honor ourselves by knowing when something is just not for us, no matter what we do. Love is not a trophy that has to be won through intense battle, blood, and bruises. Choose yourself today, and know when to stay, and when to go.

## Curtain Call

I wanted to see if your embrace felt like home
Or as if I were visiting a foreign place
A Land I used to feel secure in
Which now feels like I'm violating borders

Or my happy place where nothing else matters
Are you happy to see me home in your arms?
Or does my touch feel like a guest who has overstayed their welcome
Where are we…?

Does the bed feel like our playground
A sacred area exclusive to our bond
Or a dusty wasteland
Rusty from lack of attention

Does it feel like home in your arms?
Or more like a stranger...
Or is it stranger that this is a question at all?
Is summer setting on the fall of this connection
Is this season coming to a close
Pushing us closer to a lifetime in another timeline away from each other...

This push and pull.
This seesaw.
This back-and-forth has me confused and conflicted.
Oh, the wicked ways in which the heart is split when I was looking for wholeness with you
Perhaps that was part of the problem.
That I looked to you to fill shoes that are sitting right here
I am whole with or without you
I am home with or without you
The decision is mine on whether I allow you in it or not.

A thought so scary yet freeing
Oh, the wicked ways in which the heart is split
The self preservation spawned from desperation

Part of me says
Come closer and let me hear your deepest fears
Ones that torment your soul
Leave you thirsting for peace
I'm right here
Waiting for you to drink what you've been missing

The other part screams
Maybe that's it... We are missing.
The constant shifting on your terms.
As I ride your roller-coaster of twists and turns.
Churning my stomach.
Increasing my anxiety
And I have to get off the ride before everything I worked for is
regurgitated on the ground
In tiny bits of sickness scattered all around
a place I used to deem safe
Parts of me I handed you on a plate and asked that you handle with
care
Yet you dropped me
So maybe that's the answer I have to live with

You know those final stages where you are grieving what you once had with someone and holding onto hope that maybe things will get better? It can get so complicated because while you can see the potential, both people have to be in it and want it at the same time.

When you have intense connection with someone, it can lead to a tangled web of confusion that used to be a secure net of reassurance. It can be difficult to tell the difference. The message here is that your inner self knows what to do. Trust that the outcome works out in your best favor no matter what.

## Before You Enter...

Do not come in here giving me something to eventually get over
Do not be another reason I need to heal through pain
Do not be a disruptor to my peace
Offer a peace of mind that I can relax
And let you in

Do not come in here looking at the exits
No emergencies here
But an urgency to receive the complete you
And not have to weave through the murkiness of your past
Come in here HEALED my love
I'm willing to peel back layers and let my light touch your soul
All I ask, is you come whole...

I'm willing to learn your dark and light
But do not come in here spray hosing your plight and trauma all over
the place
Do not burn me with your singed edges
Fix that and then come get me...

But do not come in here looking for a fire extinguisher
My passion will ignite you and inspire you
But I am not here to solve what I didn't cause
I'm here to make you pause, reflect and breathe
Relieved that you can let your guard down around me
I got you - but I need safety too
Me and you against all weapons formed against us
So...we can't shoot each other.

We can't shoot each other with our past hurts and hurdles
Enlighten me with what you've learned
Show me your growth and I'll water you in impossible and unthinkable
ways you didn't know you needed

Parched parts starving for just a sip of my unique brew
I got you, but you got to get me too
So don't come in here setting me up
I've seen many games, sets and matches and it's my time to win
This looking within has me shining brighter
So don't come in here with your dimmer
Those features don't come with this package

I'm sitting here trying to salvage the discarded morsels
Scrounge them together
Glue the frayed edges with a smile
All the while
My fear has a boombox to my window
That radio is blaring ALL the old hits
All the Bullshit and I'm holding my nose
Trying to breathe life into my damaged lungs

Could you catch me when I'm on my last rung?
When my fingertips lose grip on everything I've fought for
And I slip?
Can you handle this?

No, I'm not looking for a fix
I'm searching for tiny bits
Glimmers of hope that you might be worth it
Dare to be different.
Surprise me beyond measure.
And I assure you the pleasure between us will be limitless.
Just promise me that when you do come in here.
You intend to stay…

Vulnerability is so tricky y'all. You have to let your walls down enough to be able to see over it but not all the way down too quickly so that you're not pierced by someone else's projections. It is quite a dance that we'd like to be a slow groove yet when our hearts beat faster, you can't help but want the pace to pick up.

Starting fresh with a new person, takes courage and it's not that you turn a blind eye to everything that got you here, it's just that we would love to move forward, looking through the windshield and not the rear view mirror. The key here is that both parties have done the work, know themselves, know their flaws and do their best to not make you take care of things you did not cause. As humans, we like to protect ourselves. We take tactics that we think will prevent us from ever feeling that level of pain again. The problem here is that the same way we may protect ourselves, we may be repelling love.

# Book 3: Reflecting

## The Strong Friend

I am the strong friend
I am the one who flashes a smile
Masking all the while
Struggling to get 8 muscles to work together
Such a chore when you're weathering storms no one asks you about

I am the strong friend
The one who wants everyone to be happy
Tap-dancing disguised in exhaustion
The absence of words to explain the inner turmoil
Refraining from over-sharing to the under-caring
Weight bearing down on this big heart
Built to bend but everyone has their breaking point

I am the strong friend who has gotten to that edge
The one that looks down the abyss
Over the cliff
Kicks a few pebbles to see how far they fall
Walks back to the car
And drives a few more miles in this life
Knowing the sun is on the other side of the dark days
Praying at least that sleep is a brief escape
Only to have disruption while begging for peace

I am the strong friend
The one who says 'it's fine' when it's not
The one who studies the reactions
And alters the answers to that more pleasing to the ear
Yes, some stuff is hard to hear
But imagine those words beating up against your bodies' walls
Calling for release and relief

And getting stuck because folks can't handle it
But it has to go somewhere

But right, I'm the strong friend…
Somehow appearances do exactly that
Hide
Conceal
Unless you're truly paying attention
Unless your intention is to understand
Not to land judgment on the vulnerable
Plant a flag on the nose you look down from
Taking an uninformed stance
Misplacing insights in shoes you've never walked in

I'm the strong friend who has lived several lifetimes
Several timelines
Having to erase and start over
Having to cut off in order to grow
Purge in order to really know myself
Sit beside and inside myself
Look around and re-evaluate

You'd never know how many times that edge looked attractive… To
the strong friend
Appealing even
Revealing the cracks
The secret traps leading down hallways of despair
Until logic got ahold of me
Spirit taking all control of me
Gratitude spilling out of me in rivers of tears

I could never….
take that last step over the edge
Just know the mind is intricate

And without a firm foundation in what holds you together
No one is immune
Never assume the strong friend doesn't have moments
Notice the quiet
The changes
The ranges of emotions
Just observe...
Free of analysis
Just observe....

Give the strong friend a call
A text that says 'no need to respond at all'
but I was just thinking about you
I see you
And when I don't see you, I feel YOU
I hold you in my heart and acknowledge you

Let the strong friend lay the cape down
Put it in the washer for them
Allow the soil of everyone they save
To be taken away by your love and care
Be there.

I truly believe the highly competent, seemingly put-together people are the ones who are forgotten. I call it the price of competence. In childhood, we are the kids that get told ' I never had to worry about you'.

We are the trophies, the shiny tokens of our parents' efforts. The ones that get talked about at the cookouts and reunions, yet the achievements are a glaze over what may truly be going on. The perfectionist often deals with anxiety. The upbeat one might be actually dealing with depression but can't show those wounds to our loved ones because we don't know how they would deal with the good one feeling bad.

The placater of the family wants everyone else to be happy and is conditioned to put their own needs on the shelf. So, I wrote this as a reminder that everyone needs to be checked on, not just the one who openly complains and over shares… But truly everyone.

## Heart Safety

Is my heart safe with you?
Can I take the barbed wire off
My fortress of solitude
And carve out a space just for you

Can I rest my worries on your chest
As I close my eyes and have my dreams come true
Can the way I feel be reciprocated
Presenting proof
That I've finally been through enough to have what I want

Can I trust my fears won't be exploited
But handled with care
Recognizing my fragility in taking these steps with you
I can walk on my own, I'm just asking for your hand
I'm asking for your support through the turns life throws at us

So many people are shallow
Skipping along the surface
But I'm wondering if you'd eventually venture into the deep end
with me

The questions that come to mind when you are traversing the road from like to love. While exhilarating, it can also be scary based on the level of vulnerability it takes for a true connection. This seesaw can create uncertainty, even though all evidence leads to you being in a safe situation. I can admit I have had my own spikes of anxiety from remembering past traumatic experiences, while also actively attempting to live in the now and be present. In a safe relationship, we can also become triggered by normalcy since we previously primed ourselves to expect chaos and confusion. The nervous system is constantly recalibrating yet anxiety can keep us hyper-vigilant and on guard at things that may never occur.

This reaction is a response to us wanting to protect ourselves from any further pain. All we can do is recognize that we are having that response, look for real life evidence that all is actually well. I want you to rest assured and feel confident that when something does not feel right, you will know, because now you are equipped with wisdom based on what has happened to you before. Do not be afraid to ask questions and also observe as you move closer to love. The right person will not be afraid of offering appropriate reassurance so that you both may comfortably continue building your firm foundation.

## What If...

What if a person you met

Ignited parts of you

You thought had burned out

With your broken heart


What if they tied those parts together so quickly

That you thought they were a vein of your lifeline

The puzzle piece that pulls it all together

And then they're gone....

They say people come into your life for a reason, season or lifetime. Occurrences can happen so quickly and unexpectedly that our heads are spinning. Earth has angels all around and it rings true that we are sent people along the way, that are meant to help and propel us into a deeper realm of understanding ourselves and others. Some remind you of your worth and once that mission has been completed, they flow out as stealthily as they came in. Thank them anyway for their time and purpose. It wasn't a coincidence.

## Full Moon

Miles away from you

Yet our moon is the same

When we look at it

We see the same fullness

Brightness

And I feel connected to you


Whenever you're feeling far away

Disconnected

Disjointed

Melancholy

Remember when our eyes gaze upon the same thing

I feel you


Look at the moon

And see me looking back at you

Marveling at how full you make me

Wondering if you get that familiar feeling

When we're together in each other's breathing space

There are times that distance can make us feel so far away from each other. Connection can be intoxicating which urges us to crave more and more of the other person to fill us up. If ever there's a time you feel lonely, remember that there's an interconnectedness to the sun and moon that you both share. Know there are moments when you are looking at the same thing even if you don't know it. Know there are moments you are vibrating on the same frequency, similar to listening to the same radio station and find comfort that you may be on that person's mind as well.

## Seasonal Shifts

And with the fall, we fell apart
Everything we built on the spring leaves
The green supporting our summer dreams
Frolicking on the beach
Just for our memories to erode as the seasons change
What irony that as the leaves turn
You did as well
Like entering the Equinox
Made our foundation blocks crumble

And here I am holding dead leaves
Cleaving to old laughs
Pleading with the past to become present again
For this present to gift us and regift us days, into weeks and months
For the future to be a gift I can see presently
Oh, but the hesitancy blinded by current reality
You're not here

I could print our photos out to keep me warm this winter
But there's nothing like the brush of heat
Tickling me
Teasing me like a sunset fleeing over the horizon
You know it's there, yet you always want to be closer
While night falls
And the chill of winter freezes our momentum
into a hibernating halt
I can't help but wonder
when Spring comes
Will you come around too?

You all know that saying regarding people being in our lives for a reason, season, or lifetime? It can be extremely disappointing when you see a lifetime with someone, yet they were only meant to be here for a season. I think the more frustrating part is when those things are not on the same page, for example, you envision a lifetime and they only see you as a reason – a flash in time.

You may have even put a lifetime of work into a season and feel depleted. Sit with your feelings though, there's a grieving process to losing a connection that has no blueprint. Please understand that the effort you put into someone will not go unnoticed by God. Keep showing up as authentically as you can, and the right person will reciprocate with ease.

## A Binding Thread

Sex is an invisible string
How can it not be attached
When your souls tie together like this
When your bodies fold into one another
Like the perfect ingredients of a favorite dish

This, can't possibly be no strings attached
When the heart is on the end of it
When emotions blow logic into oblivion
When the chemistry creates a new equation that cannot be reversed
When it hurts to imagine
Or fathom their absence
That complimentary piece that added to your wholeness

How silly are we to think we are wired this way
That wires don't get crossed
Whilst mixing our energy with another

How silly to think we are exactly the same
When their imprint is stamped on the very parts that bring life
The gentlest of environments
The warmest of welcomes
And we wonder how come it's hard to let go

They are forever with us
The connection doesn't change
We just change what we may do with it
But the strings...are there
The strings... are a story
A secret
A language made by you both
For you both
That can't be translated by anyone

I am aware that there are two sides to this. On one hand I am cognizant that some people can engage in intimacy without their feelings being brought into it. They can see it as a casual event meant to be fun and nothing else. I have also come across individuals where emotions and intimacy cannot be separated, especially if they have mental connection and other positive traits in common. So, the concept of 'no strings attached' definitely does not apply to all. It is case by case, considering also what each party wants out of the interaction.

If I approach this from a spiritual sense, energy matters. When you intertwine energy on a sexual level, it is inevitable that strings gravitate and merge over time. I wrote this because it was clear that some people have a blind spot to how impactful these interactions can be for both parties. You can try to excuse away and compartmentalize these events but eventually, without mature conversations, things can get confusing very quickly. Without understanding the intensity of sexual connection, you can deceive yourself into thinking it's nothing. But when you truly grasp the gravity of joining the centers of your universes with another person, you understand how powerful it can be. Keeping this in mind, my guidance for you is that you are careful with who you choose to be this close with, for there can be lasting effects beyond that moment in time.

## Toxic

This word keeps following me around...
Chasing me straight into a mirror
Through a two-way glass

Toxic.
Too much of something unnecessary
Too little of something important
An explosion of chemicals that don't mix
An implosion of emotions you can't fix
A stirring of ingredients that don't blend
A series of events we can't mend

Toxic
Five letters that urge one to do better
Know better
Five letters wrapped in regret
Stripped of progress
Slipping completely down the steps
And looking up to see how far we have fallen
We don't have to succumb to our injuries
Those wounds that we don't let others see
Yet we act from them, knowingly and unknowingly.

Toxic.
Five letters thrown around like a hot potato.
No one wants to take the blame.
Claim they didn't know what they were doing.
While repeating it over and over again.

Toxic.
An acid that burns to the touch
A crutch that lacks accountability

A fire we shouldn't get close to
Yet, we cover ourselves with it at night.
Scorching our fingertips.
Flinching and acting surprised.

Toxic
Ingesting their lies and wondering why our stomachs ache
Confused on why the bruise won't fully heal
Picking at it while complaining that it hurts
Peeping the discrepancies, but not at first

Toxic
Seeing the remedy that is age-old and proven.
Fighting with God while he's trying to remove them
Soothe us with a tonic of boundaries and standards yet
We are holding out hope.
Eyes closed to the truth, staring right back at us.

Toxic.

Do you ever get tired of your own mess? Sometimes we can be fully aware of our actions yet walk in the same direction as if we cannot foresee and predict the outcome. The word 'toxic' is thrown around for folly yet there are souls getting deeply hurt by people who are actively operating at a vibration that causes damage.

While we can get lost in a mentality of "if you can't beat them, join them" that's not a progressive action that gets us anywhere. Now, I am not sitting on a moral high horse, looking down at individuals that are not living in their highest self. I am simply pointing out that even if the masses have given up on standing up to their full power, you do not have to succumb to settling. There is no need for you to dumb down your actions so that you belong when in fact, you could be carrying a light that is meant to guide others. What if you were chosen to be the lighthouse and because you're trying to conform to the toxicity that is running rampant, you miss your purpose?

This is just food for thought as you reflect on your own potential contributions to the mess that you complain about. Choose what side you are on, and as much as you can, take ownership and accountability as you strive to do better. Together we can gain momentum that takes us out of a collective misery and messaging that people cannot change. Start with yourself and watch the world change around you. What does not belong will fall off, which is a tonic that can bring us all to a space of healing and higher purpose.

## A Long Road of Pondering

I question my journey often
The absence of ease
With my pleas to God to
Leave me out of the next war
My deployments have been plenty
And I'm near empty on fuel to keep driving through these walls

I drudge through the mud
Wiping tears with bloody hands from
Climbing up these rugged mountains
Somehow, I'm bound to a determination that can't be my own
I hone in on the whys and what's
The what ifs and buts
And all I can do is trust there's a reason for all of this.

I keep my eyes open, so I don't miss the message and the purpose.
Furthering my understanding that this is bigger than me.
The burden placed on me is so the bloodline after me is lighter
The fighter in me marches forward.
But I'm tired
While true I may be wired for intensity
A propensity for pushing through despite of
I invite and cry daily for a flow where I can float
Be at peace
And release all that's weighing me down

My vow on this winding road
Is that I help someone else glean the lessons
Extract the reasons
Without needing to endure each painful season
For that alone...
I get up
I show up
And keep walking

It's true that we are all placed here for a specific and predestined reason. While not all of us are on a journey to enlightenment where we realize our purpose, there are a few of us that take several hits and have the bruises to show for it. There are a few of us that have no choice but to be beaten and broken down to dust so that we may emerge as a light in this world.

This torch is not given to everyone and honestly there are days I do not wish to carry it. I have come to understand that my stories and challenges encourage others. While in the midst of the storms, many things do not make sense, it's inevitable that at the end of that trial, it tends to become clearer. If I can walk through some forests first, clearing a path that has less thorns and brush for the next, I know I am standing in my purpose of guiding the blind through my evolved lenses.

# Book 4: Love and Longing

## Curious Inquiries

Can I float around your mind?
View the scenery
Settle in...
And explore your depths
I'm sure even the shallow portions may amuse me
Bemusing that I'm intrigued by every piece of you

But...
Would you allow me to dive into your darkness
With you as my guide
Show me what's under the shells
I promise to treat your truth like a magnificent pearl
You can trust me
I know you'd have to trust that first...

So... your pace is fast enough
I imagine your ocean is boundless
Resounding against nothing but the walls you imprison yourself in
I can handle it
Cradle you with care
Hug you in moments you feel unlovable
You are so much more than you think

Tell me when to hold my breathe
As you exhale into me
Let life stand between us

Often in the beginning stages of meeting someone, both parties can have their guard up. People have plenty of reasons that they hold their words, thoughts, emotions close to the chest however, over time there can be an increasing desire to truly know their ins and outs. The poem above is a question, a gentle inquiry into the intricacies of another. What makes them tick? What turns them on?

There is so much to learn, and at times the excitement can be very overwhelming as you want to know everything. The question in the air is a subtle prodding that they let you in a bit more as you maintain a stance of safety and curiosity. It is natural to want to ask your person of interest, questions and with this neutral space of wonder and anticipation, the possibilities can be vast. May your exploration be fun and fulfilling.

## A Cautionary Plea

If you touch me once
I'll crave your closeness for eternity
If your burn into me with your passion
I'll crash without you next to me

Distance yourself accordingly
Until you are ready to receive all of me
For I…
Am not just a drop in the bucket
I'm a deluge raging rapidly
Pushing through limits of this levee
Brimming and overflowing
Anticipating the moment where
There's no space between us

Where
It's imminent that once we melt into each other
We are no longer the same
We are sweeter.

If one of your love languages is physical touch, there's not much explaining I need to do here. This is about the tension between two people where it is abundantly clear that there is chemistry, however you haven't quite explored those dimensions. The imagination plays out scenes that have yet to come to life and even that is exciting. With certain people, you just know, there will be an uncharted explosion of passion.

What I am describing is not from a lustful or carnal space; I am describing a mental stimulation, built on emotional intimacy that undeniably spills over sensually. Plainly, this is one of those 'alright now, watch yourself' instances where you are not warning someone per se, but there is a smirk and playfulness to the caution you are noting. You are noting that if they get close to you in an intimate way, they just may like it here.

## Fleeing into Peace

I wanted to escape into him
Open his chest up
And be as close to his heart as humanly possible
I wanted to wrap his skin around mine
Feel the security of his warmth
And not face the world

I wanted his heartbeat to lull me to sleep
Rock me to a fantasy place that feels safer than here
I wanted... rest
I wanted... peace
And for those few moments
Nothing else mattered but inhales
Exhales
And contentment

If I could have bottled that feeling up
Captured the beauty of nothingness and fullness
I would have
If I could have freeze-framed this clip
And forever remember this simplicity
I would have

All I could do is sigh
Tell myself it's okay
As his embrace told me the same without speaking at all

On a bad day, all we need is a hug. A firm, all-encompassing hold that can release the days' tension in minutes. I am certain we have all had days where words escape us, but we know we need something; a need that we cannot vocalize. There's something in your loved one's presence that speaks volumes above verbs. Our brains may be depleted and feel jumbled yet there is such grounding in an embrace where you do not have to talk. We are not meant to walk through life alone and my hope for you is that you are gifted with someone that can anticipate your needs, tell you to bring it in, wrap their arms around you, allowing you to melt into them.

## Secretly Speaking

He doesn't know...
He doesn't know the last thing on my mind
Before slumber
Adjacent to dreams
Is him.

He doesn't know
In those initial stirrings of my mind
After sunrise
Before the rush
My musings meet me with thoughts of him

It's not obsession
It's a recollection of the happiness brought into my world
By his presence
I lean over to 'his' side of bed
And breathe in our memories
The passionate delicacies of this budding love story
I inhale...possibilities
And exhale a sigh of peace

He has no idea
That there's so much behind this gaze
I study him
Making mental images of everything I enjoy about him
*click*
A glimpse of a slight twinkle when he's amused
*click*
The smoothness of his melanin
*click*
That dimple when he smiles
*click*

That grounded breathing all the while
I'm struggling to keep my heartbeat from bursting under his touch

It's damn near overwhelming to feel…this.
The kiss that tells me things he isn't saying
I hear you.
That embrace that wraps all the way around my frame
I feel you.
I know…and you know…
We understand the unspoken
We may even overanalyze the hope then
When we are in front of each other, all the worry withers away
The slow burning energy between us lets me know it's okay
I rest my mind and let your soul find me in the ethers
It's possible it was written just like this
And the joy is in the discovery of this unexpected bliss

Have you ever felt so strongly about someone that you were afraid of the feelings you were experiencing? Feeling uncertain about what to verbalize or keep to yourself, there can be an inner dialogue that you have with yourself. Falling in love does not need to be chaotic or an intent rush of emotion, for it can also be a slow and subtle charge that is ever-present when you are around that person. Like softly playing music that serves as a soundtrack for your quality time. Similar to sipping wine, savoring the hints of fruit and flavor, you are attempting to slow down and take in each moment in digestible pieces.

It can be hard to catch your breath when someone is so captivating in your gaze and embrace. Do yourself a favor and engage all of your senses into your time with them. What new characteristic do you notice in their features? Take in the way they look at you, how does it feel? Immerse yourself in their voice when they are speaking to you. How does their skin taste under your lips? Is your nose pleased by their scent? Does your body perk up at the merest brush of their arm against yours? Notice what is activated by this connection and be grateful for being in this moment. Take nothing for granted, because all you have is the now.

## He is Home

He is home…
Not that he has arrived but when I arrive to him I know I am safe
His embrace feels like contradiction to my history
A statement of commitment I can't ignore
A declaration that he will be different
A blanket that won't be ripped away from me

Home feels like...
A consistent relaxation
A unspoken peace resting between pauses and touches
The end to my questioning sentences
Wondering what if
How come
And why now.

He quiets All of that with his kisses
He silences those embers within me that carry doubt, worry and fear
I hear his secure voice above my negative chatter
Each caring touch reinforces the feeling that
I am wanted
I am valuable
I am loved

Home feels like...
My favorite meal other people just could not get right
The spices were off
The center was overcooked
And in that, my needs were overlooked
Overshadowed by other's preferences and references to
who hurt them before me
Making my new role an uphill battle
With no manual nor blueprint
Just a footprint of who stomped on his heart
With treads and trauma running deep

My natural touch raw to his skin
Foreign to feeling safe

But within this home we are building with each other
He covers me in comfort
Caresses my insecurities
Emotional intimacy weaving a new quilt of surety
And trust.

My shell cracks with each tender word spoken
Poking at my shyness
Prying my barbed wire I so delicately placed
Around my soft, vulnerable spaces others mishandled
Fumbled
Stumbling just short of the end zone

But he... he touches down deep
Verbally massaging scar tissue I deemed forever bruised
Intentionally he chooses to see through
And view me at a purity only kindred souls can understand

I rest content
Softened and feminine
Slumbering at a level only an untroubled mind can achieve
A reprieve from having to stand on guard
At unexpected wars and tours I didn't sign up for
But with him I nestle into uncharted relaxation
Elation that I too, can wake up to
A cozy home of hopeful anticipation
A foundation I'm excited to decorate in compassion, fun and gratitude
He is home...

Have you ever searched for an apartment or home and though the space met some of your criteria, checking most of your boxes, it still did not 'feel right'? Because the spaces did not quite satisfy all of your wants and needs, you keep hoping to find a home that truly suits you. When you find that ideal place, you can start to look around and naturally ideas come to mind involving how you will decorate and where the furniture will go; suddenly it all makes sense without you having to force it.

That is what a home should be and though that's an ideal situation, I do feel that with the world taking shots at us daily, relationships with a person should feel like home. A place you can rest your head without having to keep one eye open. I believe feeling like home with a person can be akin to you naturally seeing where your furniture would fit, which room you would make memories, how it would feel to entertain guests there. You would not have to stretch your mind in unreasonable ways to 'see it'. My hope for you, is that you create a home with someone worthy of all that you bring.

## Remembering His Presence

I wake up and roll to my right
Remembering, just a week ago
My head rested in one of my favorite places that feels like home.

My ear catching your heartbeat
While grounding mine in gratitude
It's those quiet moments
Intangible
Unexplainable
That I can't get enough of

Joy trickles down my face
Moistens my cheeks
And I just… sigh

I blink, take a mental snapshot
Of this very moment of peace
So that when I wake up alone
I can recall *this*
And remember your touch
Is just a thought away....

When exploring a connection with someone, their physical presence can leave an imprint on you. The memories can feel like movies that highlight the best parts of your time together. Some of the sweetest moments can occur in silence where you are soaking up the experience; how they smell, how they feel, and how they are starting to have an effect on you.

It's important to not rush through these moments and take inventory of the way you feel just breathing next to them. Do you feel peaceful? Are you relaxed? Is your nervous system at ease? Are you embracing the moment or looking too far ahead and missing out on the beauty in this current room? Breathe. Deeply. Remember 'this'. When you find yourself missing that person, and wishing you were next to them right now, allow your mind to go back to that morning and sift through each fulfilling and comforting detail. Let that relax you until you can see them again.

## Warm Memories

I thought about you upon my awakening
As the sunrise tickled my eyelids
Bright flashes of your touch stimulated my senses
The warmth that radiates from your heart to mine
created a glow that played at the corners of my mouth
And poured over my entire being

A naturally refreshing reaction
A hope washing over my pain
Receding and eroding over failed foundations
Anticipation of a new beginning
Housed in a double Dutch-like stop and go
yet my goal is to flow and
Meet you in the wind
Let this budding love carry us into unknown and uncharted bliss

Your kiss propels me into fantasies of forever
However this history nudges my psyche and I pause
I wonder if this will be new
Or an old brew I've tasted before
Sour to my tongue
Bitter in remembrance of another not receiving
This bruised but not broken heart

But this start feels like…. We could finish?
Like this story has… an inspiring end
Like…we pave a path others follow and then
Show them how it's done
Show them that staying the course has its reward
And it's oh so sweet
That a love like this melts like cotton candy
Slowly dissolving

Seeping through and around our taste buds
Instantly yearning for more…..of this.
Damn near addictive how the best parts of you trickle
To pieces I didn't know needed flavor
Yet, here you are
In all of your glory
Just being You.
And I thank you for reviving the possibilities
That you and me, could be…
Us.

I've always said that matters of the heart are not math. Some things just don't make sense, however there are times your higher self just knows that someone is for you. Meeting someone's soul still requires so much work in the body and flesh and although we may know things to be true, there's still a journey to be walked here on Earth.

This is about walking through pain and fiercely refusing to allow your history to be your future. There's such a bravery with trying again and again. My encouragement to you is that it can happen. Do not give your past the power to dictate how you move forward. Heal. Learn from it. Use the lessons and equip yourself for what you deserve.

## Mind Stimulation

Seduce me with your conversation
Melt my heart with your words
Soothe my wound with your secure embrace
Assure my inner child you're here to stay

Trace my back with your tender tickles
Cup my curves and don't let go...
Show me how much you've missed me

Breathe with me for a bit...
Breathe in me for a bit...
Breathe me in for a bit...
Sip my oasis I've saved just for you

Search no longer, for this is where destiny landed us
Let's listen to our vibrations match
Watch our frequencies wrap ribbons around our hearts
Take your time telling me what you've been thinking
I'm wide open to catch your fears

By now, it should be no secret that when a woman is mentally stimulated, the effects can trickle down. This formula does not apply to everyone however, more times than not this is what I have noticed. The exploration of someone new, hopefully involves communication and curiosity. The beginning stages of learning someone should be fun!

As you dive deep into each other's minds, it can breed a very strong intrigue that strings together those initial threads of connection. Savor it and take your time, for you may be experiencing exactly what you've asked for. Listen with your mind, body and spirit. You will know if it is for you, but again, I reiterate, have fun with the process. Let the beat build for a minute and take in the complete harmony of your interactions.

## Reminiscent Heat

You remind me of a summer love
That "when can I see you again" love
That warm sunset, holding hands love
You remind me of an easier time
Where lines were clear and the moments were so dear
That you wish you could stretch those moments
and make them last forever
Tickling my skin with your warm gaze
feeling like the most beautiful sunset

You remind me of a summer love
Fleeting and meaningful
Like a newly released one hit wonder
Everything plays a part
And for that season you held my heart in a way I'll never forget

Promise you'll never go away
Or at least shine bright in my memories
Stay present when I close my eyes
Grant me a stay in that corner of your heart
I regret nothing, except that summer is only one season.
As the days get shorter, I can also feel our time could be narrowing
Though I ache at sunset
I can't help but be grateful for you making some of my days bright
Enlightening my understanding of being present.
And living in the now

Everything is not meant to last forever, and that can be a difficult concept to reconcile. In the middle of a connection, the euphoria can be so intoxicating that you begin to imagine long-term potential. One of the most important aspects of a connection is answering the question surrounding if both people want the same level of depth; and at the same time.

Chemistry is one component of a relationship however it can boil down to stages of readiness and willingness to agree to meet each other's needs on a consistent basis. In this piece, I explain a nostalgia that would make anyone smile and marvel at memories yet a bittersweet nature that even the best of summers, come to a close.

# Book 5: Protecting

## Scar Tissue

Though you have been hit with challenges
That have rocked you to your core.
I assure you that you will not be forever broken

You may be sensitive to the touch.
The surface may feel rough
As you navigate life with a new wound
But I can assure you that you will not be forever broken
Nor soaking in the sorrows of your battles
Like scar tissue that eventually forms around the gash
This pain and rawness will not always last.
Each day you show up for yourself
You are affirming that you can heal

New flesh is connecting to help you move forward
Through
Around
The sound of your tears is not falling on deaf ears
Each droplet hitting the sore spot
Is cleansing that tender area
The one you hide while crumbling inside

It is being strengthened
Cell by cell
Layer by layer
Until you have a healthy barrier
That doesn't look the same
But works just as well

That's wisdom and lessons
Regret and transgressions gathering around your bruise
So, when you look down at it
A more guided path you may choose

Scar tissue protects us with a reminder
Of what we've been through
But it's not meant to punish or condemn
It's a gentle nod and wave
To what once emitted intense throbs
And your heart beats a new melody
This scar tissue is meant to tell you
That you have survived 100% of your hardest days
That you are not just meant to stumble over the finish line
But that you are destined to soar and let nothing hold you back

It is true that we have not asked for the multiple battles we've endured. On the other hand, we need not pigeonhole ourselves, stamping a label onto our existence where we are defined by our pain. Even though you have experienced several harsh events, you do not have to mentally stay there. You can acknowledge what happened while not ruminating on why it went that way. Circling back and repeating those awful moments will not help you move forward. Many times, it actually exacerbates the pain as your mind and body revisit that event in all of its graphic details.

Like a tape that is stuck on pause, you need not stay stagnant in the story of what happened to you. As you move through your healing process, you can ask yourself a few questions to gain momentum on the road to relief. What did you learn about yourself and others based on this event? Is there a theme within yourself that you need to examine? Is there anything that you would've done differently, if you had the chance to do it again?

For the events where they were completely out of your control, the above questions can feel more difficult since you did not cause the trauma. In this case we can lament over questions like 'why did this person do this', 'why did they treat me this way' and though you may find a place of understanding that other person's actions, there is still work on your end to prevent their past actions from governing your future. This is the only thing you are in control of; how you respond thereafter. The virtual scars from these events do not have to leave such a mark that you cannot find a way forward. Your mission and gift to yourself is to blaze a trail, a path that keeps going, despite anything that has come before now.

## A Petition for Connection

Social media is ruining us
Grooming us to be pierced with what is immediate
Fierce loyalty to something so fleeting
Addicted to what is instantly gratifying
Satisfying the present
While stealing from the future
Aspirations oozing out of our retinas
and swooping up a plethora of lost ideas

Stuck in a screen
Ravening down a spiral of lights, camera and action
All for a reaction and a laugh
While loved ones are crying in a corner
dying to be seen
To be revered with the same excitement
A delight when the eyes can lock in on each other
A deep focus on what's in front of you
yearning for acknowledgment

Life is not pending nor loading…
It is ever-changing and unfolding in real time
While true connections freeze
Waiting to be unthawed by active engagement
A warmth that is unmatched to the static nature of an inanimate
object

Life is meant to be lived fully in action
In intention
Life is meant to be lived in the silence between spaces of constant
stimulation
We are missing so much by touching the screen more than we are
touching each other.

How can we recover from the void of minimal connection
When we prioritize what's out there versus what's right here
We urgently need to steer back into what is truly important.
And return to stealing moments that can only be caught with eye
contact and unplugging

Time is tugging and pulling at us second by second
And before we realize it
It is too late to regain what we have been missing out on
Because our attention was on the wrong things

We are increasingly glued to what jumps out in front of us that we forget to look at what was there the whole time. We are losing key moments because our attention is split and it's leading to half listening, and more misunderstandings, as well as a growing feeling of neglect in our interactions. My call to action here is that we train ourselves to be mindful of our on-screen time and remember to be fully present in our real-life experiences. Between being overwhelmed, and overstimulated by feeds and timelines, it's possible we are starting to be underserved and disappointed by our loved ones. This is especially true if one of your love languages is quality time which includes undivided attention. It can feel like a slap in the face to someone who is yearning for full engagement to build emotional intimacy.

While I know social media is not all bad, and can truly be utilized for amazing causes, my commentary is geared towards the mindless scrolling that we do, looking for constant dopamine hits. I think we are starting to be conditioned towards needing constant highs and are missing aspects where we need to sit with ourselves and be present to others. If this resonates with you, take some time to examine any areas where you may want to improve the ways you spend your time, especially if other people are around. Take a tally over the course of one day of how many times you are drawn to pick up your phone and see if you can connect it to a feeling, whether that be boredom, seeking distraction, or something you may not be aware of yet. This tiny moment of reflection can be a start to improving your in-person interactions, and on a larger scale, bring us back to what matters most.

## The Blueprint

I'm not someone you test drive
Take around the block and see how fast I go
I am a buy on-site type of specimen
With a tempo so groovy I make
Your heart beat my name

The sane choice
Is not to think too long
Not to study and still get it wrong
You already know what I bring
The radio sings my frequency
And I vibrate high
Low hanging fruit isn't suited here
The patterns don't lie…

And neither does my authenticity
A BS detector so keen
You'll want to hide words you haven't thought of yet
See, the truth is the only trait I invite freely
The root of your being is what I'm seeking
So, buyer beware…
There's a full package to consider
Before you sit in this chair

Before you shift all the mirrors
Make sure you can see Yourself clearly
When you get in front of me
I'll hold your heart dearly
But I'm heavy on the accountability
And I don't hold back on the transparency
You're getting… ME.

I offer specs not listed on the stats
It ain't for everybody
But I promise you…
I'm more than a stroke of luck
Of course I know the perfect word that rhymes with luck
But
I'm classy

Blast up these tunes with me
And let's get lost in a love story
Travel some roads with me and
Let me hear your journey

Hug my curves around your blind spots
I got you
Take your hands off the wheel when you're tired
I'll spot you
I'm here…
If life veers us down an unexpected path
Know, I'm here to keep us straight
Your maintenance of me governs
How long it takes before I break
I'm handing you the manual
It's your choice to make

Good and well-intended souls often meet the unhealed ones who end up sucking them dry. It may be unintentional, but it's still causing damage and havoc to the people who have already taken their journey. There can be lasting effects on those that have done the work and are ready for conscious loving experiences.

When considering exploring dating and relationships, please take a self-assessment regarding your true readiness. I believe we can all do ourselves a favor when we take a deep look at ourselves and be as honest as we can. What I am speaking of in this poem is a cautionary plea that many folks have, and it stems from disappointment when they have met someone that only wanted bits and pieces of them vs. the full beauty of all they had to offer. This is a collective cry of exasperation when two people are not on the same page, even if it was initially presented that way.

There are so many great people out here that are emotionally unavailable and present at a level where they can welcome in a relationship and have it flourish. But when the good and well-intended souls meet the unhealed ones, there is a mismatch that can be extremely aggravating for the person who is showing up consistently, and with full effort.

So as humanity, we need to help each other out. This war within connections and situationships needs to move closer to a feeling of being on the same team, with the same goal. Right now, the healed hearts are getting broken, and the broken hearts are blindly perpetuating more cycles of pain. If we can come to an understanding that at a base level we are desiring love, connection, and to do life with people who add to our lives and not subtract, we would do our own work first before approaching others. As a hopeful romantic, that is my hope and prayer for us all.

## The Straw

Thank you for the straw
It broke the camel's back
My heart
My trust
My restoration of faith in humanity
It broke...everything

But without it, I wouldn't move
I wouldn't prove to myself that I could actually make it
Without this
This thing that kept me tethered
The hope I piled onto empty excuses and broken promises
The thing I wanted to show my parents
That we'd be better
That we'd remember their struggle and dare not repeat it

But I'm realizing the defeat is in repeating the same grievances
And thinking it will be different
Oh the hypocrisy that we are made with 50% of our parents'
personalities
And think we are immune to rinsing and repeating some shit
oh the hypocrisy...that we judged their choices and made the same
Maybe even worse

It's a tragedy, but thank you for the straw
That thing I could never recover from without admitting I am weak
That last thing that decided my heart's future
That one aspect that killed us and any plans
To be us vs them
To run a Boston on these mofos that thought we had no spades
No trade options, just you and me
Only to find out your secret weapon was me

From those tired nights you couldn't utter a word
You got a back rub
To the times you didn't know what you needed, but I did.
And gave it to you
No one but us, saw the marathon conversations with minimal to
moderate gain
While the investment was so mountainous
So meaningful
That we'd do all of them over again if we had to

But that straw...
You did that
You hid that between the smiles and charm
Undoing harm with each backpedaling statement
It's not that I didn't have a clue....
And I guess that's why I sit here
Not crying, not lamenting, not even upset
But just...at peace
Thank you for the straw

We have all been there. The grief that comes along before the actual end of a relationship. We ponder what will be that last event that pushes you over the edge you had been hanging onto so tightly. Many times, that edge is a blind spot to the other person involved, and they may even improve their efforts when you are already gone. When one is at peace with the decision they are about to make, there's actually a calm that washes over you. That calm feeling knowing you've exhausted all options and have rationalized plenty of excuses, yet the reality remains that sometimes you have to part ways. Sometimes the damage is so severe that it is irreparable, and the only thing you can do is save yourself. That straw is subtle and unexpected; it drops so loudly because it holds that minute morsel of hope.

Similar to grief, there can be a relief that things are over. The tension in your stomach lessens, the overthinking through each aspect lands you at the same revelation. Some things and people must go. We have to decide whether it's more painful to hold onto something that is unfulfilling or experience the temporary pain of letting it go. Amid the confusion, many of us believe it will be more painful to let it go. But when our hands are free of the worry and baggage, we can willingly and openly welcome the new and better.

# Book 6: Healing

## A Cleansing Release

Let these tears slough off the remainder of this pain

May they travel a road to freedom and exploration

Let the door close on my sorrow

For tomorrow is a new day

Healing through painful experiences can also include crying. Crying can be cathartic and cleansing. I have met individuals who do not allow themselves to cry, for they see it as a sign of weakness vs. a response that is helpful to feeling better. This is one of those instances where, one may be afraid to sit with uncomfortable feelings, but I can say this often makes it worse.

When we avoid our emotions, we likely prolong our suffering. Strength comes in all forms, including sadness, as there is an honoring of the feeling that allows us to be present and emotionally available to ourselves. The more we can identify our emotions and responses, the better we can relate to others. Crying is okay and can be just the release we need.

May this chapter assist you on matters that may be hard to address. Examine your pain points and identify what still feels sore. As you absorb the following chapter, my purpose is to relate to you, as we have all had challenges we have had to work through. You deserve to move this pain to a space where you don't forget it, but it is not the lens in which you view and interface with the world.

## A Fallen Angel

When an empath doesn't care

You must have really taken them there

Stretched their limits of compassion

Until it's a passing fancy of interest

Turned to apathy

When an empath doesn't care

Just know that the well is dry

You have drained out more than you poured in

Such a sin to affect someone with boundless heart space

You really must have did them in

Those who know me have probably heard me describe being an empath as someone with a dotted line around them vs. a solid one. What I mean by that is, when someone is intuitive and perceptive, they generally have a nature that is nurturing to others. They may also have a deeper understanding of humanity and their purpose in life. The ones that walk around with this kind of light are often the same individuals who are misused and taken advantage of because their light attracts unhealed souls. But even one with empathic nature has limits, and in fact, has to set stronger boundaries, since we are naturally wired to overaccommodate and overextend ourselves to the needs of others. Since we are spiritual beings immersed in a human experience, the human side of us can get downtrodden with the plight of others and what I've seen is that being understanding can have a liability and you can lose yourself. When I speak of an empath, not caring it is not stemming from a lack of compassion, it's the exhaustion manifesting into disappointment, when our efforts and love are not reciprocated.

If you identify as someone with an empathic and intuitive nature, it will be exceedingly necessary for you to understand your limits, and to advocate for your needs since your natural default may be to put yourself last. As a former people- pleaser, I can say it may be challenging at first to set those boundaries, however the more practice you get from checking in with yourself, truly asking yourself what is best for you, it will get easier. Your mind, body, and spirit will thank you over and over again.

## Toxic Math

I gave all of me
You gave half of you
That math ain't been right for some time
Mixed numbers
Mixed fluids
Integers not dividing right
Because that wasn't the original plan
You being the common denominator
Wasn't supposed to dominate me...

Yet here I am...well-rounded
Trying to make a square have softer edges and flow with me
That work isn't mine anymore
It never was
You came in masked in niceties
Swearing you were different
Declaring I was the one
That I was the sun in your world
So how in the hell did I end up revolving around you?
Such trickery of the mind when the soul is tied to
Lies and deceit

Refusal of defeat
Such a feat to rise above the noise
Ascend beyond the chatter
Gray matter destined to makes things unclear
But here I am
Seeing it for what it is
Got the red out
Resurrected the dead out of my confusion
Awakened by the pure white light that was always within me
I may have given all of me

While you gave half of you
But today I take it all back
So I can be whole again
Never to lose my full self in half truths
Ever again…

This right here is called "Done". There's no poetic way to further express the point of exasperation that is listed above. This is also called the 'point of no return' where you may be in the stage of grief that involves anger. When I've experienced anger about a relationship ending, I've also pointed the finger at myself for how much I tolerated. I wonder if you have ever been there, friend.

Love and connection runs deep, and when deception is involved, there can be several layers to untangling your emotions. When that moment of clarity comes, it can crystallize all the pieces that did not make sense before and once you get to this level of acceptance, is when the true healing begins. It is perfectly natural to have a jumbled ball of emotions and visceral responses when working through a loss. Please know you will not feel this way forever and that others can help you, should you find yourself stuck in any of these phases. You do not have to walk this healing journey alone.

## A Wish to Rewind

I miss the feeling right before
Right before I found out it was a lie
The illusioned comfort I felt
Swimming in ignorance
Blissfully kissing deception in its mouth

I miss the murk-less lenses
When my view didn't have a gray cast over it
When the pinks, and oranges made life seem brighter
Even if it was a façade

I miss being swept in the fantasy that I was immune to such pain
Frolicking around in an unscathed mind
Insulated in the padding of betrayal
A fabric so thick, I couldn't see my way out
Oh, the care taken to keep the wool over my eyes
The protection from my heart being shattered

Man, I could see how being blind brings joy
Though fake, we can create the best imaginary scenes
In front of the green screen

How I envy the ones who haven't met Oz…
The hope breathing life into each step
The anticipation that one can fix it all
All for it to fall flat
Revealing the flawed cogs and sprockets
Barely holding it together

Take me back
No, not to that….
But to a space where my walls aren't as high as mountains

Where my fountains of excitement and hope
Are overflowing and abundant
Where I can sleep with both eyes closed
Not afraid to wake up to half-truths exposed...

I want to be fully awake and present in the Now
I want my doubts to be a distant, far away memory in never neverland
Because never never, would a person stomp on my heart
While I hold theirs in the gentlest of care
Never never, would someone fumble the most beautiful story and
make it a nightmare
Never never, would my divine partner
Look directly at my pain, with a double mask
And still infect me with their poison

Oh yeah yeah I know
Never say never
But this vision is clear
I have laser focus, Eyes on the prize
And my time is here

Nothing can make me go back to that
I don't fit anymore
The door is painted shut and bolted
As I folded on this game
Knowing the pot was too toxic for me
And my sanity is no longer up for sale

So today....
I say never
Never will I shoot myself in my own heart
Based on fantasies, I created by what someone tells me
Meanwhile, they are dancing in their own unresolved pain
The betrayal wasn't only him

It was me too
I betrayed myself and that crime costs way more
Than any deceit someone could project on to me
We have to reject the notion
That our circumstances are due to outer explosions
In fact, it's a turmoil and implosion when we don't see our own worth
When we don't do our own work, once we know better
We can no longer claim victim when the curtains come crashing down
And the lights reveal all the mold
The heap of dust sitting on things we haven't addressed

When the tests are done
And we reach that final examination
That final destination of enlightenment
The highest extent of compassion and grace for ourselves
This is when we know
We have indeed Elevated

We cannot go back to before
We just have rest assured that AFTER is a mission
A call to action for us all
That with this wisdom and those lessons
We will not fall over the same hurdles again.

The deep shock and betrayal that comes from infidelity. Let's just call it what it is and be clear. It hurts and it is gut-wrenching. A story and road I wish I would never have to tell or mend my heart from. Experiencing deception like this is an intricate experience because when there's love between you two, you never imagine the same person could cause the deepest pain and loss of trust. Infidelity can unearth all of your triggers and sore spots to be exposed at once, at the moment it all comes out. Like a shock to the system, it can be quite disorienting.

In my experience, I deeply wished I could rewind my mental tape to the moments before I knew anything. So I discuss the illusion of happiness because that's what it is. That's what it was. A guise had me believing all was well. Though I believe in honesty, it made me realize why people lie. They lie to save face, and others lie to protect you… Somewhere in the middle it can be a combination of both, and other things I have not discovered.

Concerning my situation, there were several acts of selfishness that kept being revealed as time went on. The iceberg reached deeper than I had ever imagined, and the disgust I felt as I learned what he did, made me sick to my stomach. While it's not my way of operating, I can see where someone that cares about you, would not want to reveal their selfish moments. The carnage thereafter is similar to shrapnel blown all over the place and you're not sure which piece to pick up first. It all feels sharp to the touch while your emotions are raw.

I have found that it's natural to pour over the details of the past and try to tease out potential clues however, the real work is very personal and internal. The deceptive actions of someone, is not an alarm for us to rush in and fix their issues. It is a very loud nudge to make a decision that serves your best interest. Do not betray your own needs and mental health based on the transgressions of a person you cannot control. Eventually, you will resent putting your desires on the shelf.

## The Final Stop

The pain in her eyes as she looked at her past
Standing right in front of her in the present
Yet she saw no future with him

These worlds colliding made her realize
What may come next
May not have him in it

The soul was perplexed
By an idea that this meeting was meant to end
That this was written this way - and nothing could change it

The remains of this connection rested in the dead space between them
The silence
The lost moments never to return
The damage and the carnage
Rested in the dead space between them

The foundation was shattered beyond recognition
And they laid on the ashes
One last time
The embers flickered
One last time
And when they blinked themselves back to this reality
All there was…
Was smoke burning any remaining images of togetherness

This was not a see you later
They knew this was the last time
They'd see each other later
The last time this layer of lust filled the room
Painting the air with cries and sighs
A harmony disbanded by a composer

Who couldn't keep his composure enough
To stay devoted to one
A composer who created multiple symphonies
That all fell flat
Sharpened by the daggers of deceit

She laid there defeated
Knowing she sang her heart out to an empty soul
Who piled bodies around him to keep himself whole
She sweat his pipe dreamt fantasies out of her pores
Stories crafted so seamlessly
Crumbs breaded so sweetly they made her succumb
Voluntarily clung to empty promises
Strung together by temporary highs
Oh, the lies…

The dead space between them
Swung there like a noose
Ready for the next neck to bloody and bruise
And abuse
This proves….
The most brilliant of minds can be blinded
Primed and groomed

Consumed with flashing sights and sounds
You'd never assume you could be bound to an energy meant to destroy
you
A toxicity so acidic you could choke on common sense…
This lens was a viewfinder
Filled with fairytales
Burnt wedding veils
And no happy endings

This rabbit hole makes you wonder

How many holes buried his scent
Beneath these shadows.
You pray you could prevent uncertain death
Pleading one could detect a poison before there's nothing left
Hoping for an elixir to fix it all…
But this… was meant to dissipate
Only leaving behind lessons and promises to self
To Never drown in another's self-induced misery
Swimming to the shores of certainty and safety
Where no illusions reside

Second chances are acceptable until they are not. When considering whether to try again with a romantic partner, there can be a fear of revisiting prior issues that led to the original separation. I can attest to experiencing the tricky space between vulnerability and looking over your shoulder. But have you ever had an experience where you looked at a person you loved so much, and it just feels different? I describe a confusing moment where I was not sure whether my life beyond this day included him. That in itself can be hard to admit and come to grips with. Sometimes though, you just know you have reached the last stop on the train. The pain you previously endured was already too much and when you envision moving forward, you are more scared than excited.

If you have ever been in a situation like this, understand this is a point of reflection, assessing the pros and cons, risks and beyond. In circumstances that involve infidelity, there is an extra added layer of mistrust that can be difficult to rebuild without the full effort of the other person. Here is when you have to decide whether your current and future efforts and understandings will be worth it in the long run. Sometimes, it is best to accept your losses and move on, leaving them right where they are.

## That Gear

Maybe I just don't have that gear in me
That extra push that looks beyond
Crushing heartbreaks
Endless disappointments
Neverending compromises that feel like a lose-lose

I tend to choose happiness over despair
Peace over declaring years of an unfulfilled union
Just to brag numbers in the rafters
I wish to craft a genuinely abundant connection
A correction of rushed decisions
And expectations hidden behind a mask designed to prove the critics
wrong
A resurrection of our own core values
That shan't be dragged down by others' dysfunctional and irrational
scripts

We...will write this in a calligraphy of our own ink
Filled with lessons learned
And trust earned through loving communication
Sealed by a common goal of joy.
An organic longing to soak up each other's essence
Letting the comfort of secure attachment fuse our hearts together
for as long as 'ever more' allows us

Yet, I wonder if my idealism
Is a prison I've created in my mind
That at times I can't view life beyond the bars of inevitable trials
Where I'll have to stand up
Show up and consistently claim him
Even when the judge and jury swears by another verdict
Where I'll have to wrangle the gavel before it hits the block

Because the outcome is ours to decide

That gear takes grit and discretion
A discernment of what to share and what to manage within the system
I want the gears to be smooth
I don't wish to prove my worth through unrecognized efforts
Sprinkling glitter on dirt, and expecting a masterpiece
I desire a clear lane where the corners don't have unpleasant pitfalls
Causing setbacks I've already healed from
Overcome
And reconciled

I want my gears to recover from idling too high
For too long
And settle into a pace of safety that protects me for the long haul
I want my systems to feel like new....with wisdom
Forging forth on the road ahead equipped with
Hope and discernment

There is a period right after a breakup or separation, where you feel an ache of grief, and possibly also relief that something better is coming. When better is knocking at your door, you may wonder if you have full capacity to give the effort it takes for someone to get to know you. Depending on your own healing process, it can be hard to imagine that you will feel like a new person is worth what you gave the last. The biggest 'what if' though is, what if you don't? What if you don't try? Are you limiting yourself when happiness and love is on the other side? The guidance here is be gentle with yourself, and do frequent check-ins to make sure that you are honoring your needs and where you are in this journey.

In the space where you may be mending your heart, please understand that it will not feel like a straight line, and in fact, you may have intense moments of wanting to pull back with the new person out of protection. What I've found is, that we are not closed off to love; we are trying to avoid being hurt again. Since love and vulnerability is a risk and a reward, the check-ins with yourself will inform you regarding your level of readiness to open up. Do not let anyone rush your process, for anything good and long-lasting does not need to be rushed. Take your time.

# Clear it Out

I am breaking free of bitter
Desperately dashing from disappointment
In a race with myself against myself
Those old sores that bleed
outside the bandage of avoidance
Despair
And Longing

I wrap a quilt around the coldness of my heart
Hoping to warm it up to new ideas
Interactions
Yet fractions of me are divided towards this new normal
An informal introduction to being whole
And solo...
And so long as I'm piecing together fragments
Snatched away in broken promises
I wonder if my plate is as attractive
With glue mending shards
Hardening around the scar tissue left by the unhealed
My hope for 'real' seals together my broken edges
And hedges around the possibility that I too can have true love

But I am breaking free of bitter
These weeds of doubt and jadedness do not belong
anywhere near this sunflower, reaching to the sky
Being brightened by positive energy
Shining from the hearts of others that mean well
My soul swells with cautious optimism
While I consider the continuous prism of colors that life can bring me
And I am open to it all

Being open minded while navigating in the healing process can feel like a roller coaster of emotions. I truly believe that healing is not linear therefore, it will have its twists and turns that times may feel like a regression. Even if you have experienced a series of romantic interactions that have not ended in the outcome you wished, I do not wish for you to look at those situations and overgeneralize, walking away, saying "all XYZ do XYZ" or "maybe I am meant to be alone forever." It's inaccurate, incorrect, and will limit you from love and happiness you deserve. As a writer, I understand the power and weight of words so my plea for you is to not insulate yourself with statements that pigeonhole you into a negative mindset.

## Choosing a Melody

What song do I sing right now?
I could sing a song of redemption
yet I haven't arrived yet
I feel so captive to my thoughts that a song of freedom wouldn't fit
quite yet
But I'm getting there
I'm walking there, ensnared by my past
Hoping the darkness doesn't last too much longer

What song do I sing in the forest that someone can hear
What clear notes can I belt so
It can be a felt understanding that I'm about to break
Spirit, come find me before it's too late
Hear my cry to the trees
I need you
Feed me Your wisdom
Christen me with clarity
Help me see the reason you are breaking me apart
Put me back together with new threads
New treads on my shoes so I don't slip next time
Or at least when I do stumble
I don't fall so hard

We are all out here just trying to figure it out. Though we may have different compasses and motivations, it can be difficult to ask for help. In our experiences we can hit these points of uncertainty where the only thing we can do is breathe and take each moment minute by minute.

Essentially, we can get lost in the weeds of whatever we have going on and lose sight of the bigger picture. That's the plight of humanity, mastering the skill of finding balance and peace in the midst of chaos. Staying grounded while navigating challenges. We would love to sing a song of victory, yet we are still in the battle, so we may need a motto or statement we repeat to ourselves to keep us moving forward even at the tiniest of steps. Each step matters even if you are not "there "yet.

## This season

This season of isolation
It's not because you are alone
It's because you are supposed to find home
In the heart of the darkness
In the spark ignited within you that was almost blown out

Where you are searching is within you
And No one else can find it BUT you
You can reach out
Seeking the support of others
Yet this journey is yours
Forcing you to only look Up

Asking not 'why' but 'what next'
What steps are ordered while I step blindly
When I finally see the purpose behind this solo journey
When my yearning for connection
Would've delayed my direct intention to the Source
That requires this solitude to correct the course
I have to look at things this way
I have to be alone to pray
To see the lighthouse in the night when I'm frightened by my own
thoughts echoing on these walls
I call out to see if anyone is listening
And the only One who answers
Speaks to me in my dreams

So, I sleep just a little more...
Begging to be met with clarity
Sharing my desires with the only One who got it all along
Who knew my life song before I sang a note
Who proved I'm never alone even when it feels lonely

If only…
I'd listened more than I spoke
I'd have heard the message long ago
That people are temporary
Equally lost on their own paths
And sadly, the only thing we can depend on
Is that they will change
Their roads will rearrange
to fit their timeline
Combining their past and present
Redefining their future
And sometimes that means your exit is up

The gem in this reality is
This is also the way it's supposed to be
Source is course-correcting us all
And in the fall when the seasons are changing
We also are urged to renew
To be reborn
Over and over again

Some may recall the saying of "having too many cooks in the kitchen ". It is an old adage that resonates with me for several reasons. It is perfectly fine to seek support and advice from our loved ones and friends, however there are also moments where our Higher Power wants us to stand still, sit in silence, and hear what Spirit is trying to tell us. We can have too much interference that can pull us in several directions and create more confusion.

I know firsthand that isolation can feel like a punishment, and also like the opposite of what you feel you need. It can be extremely uncomfortable when you're at a breaking point and craving relief. Please remember that you may experience moments where it feels like everything and everyone is being stripped away, it may help you to see that as a moment where you have a direct line to the Source. Moments like this force you to activate your intuition and listen for divine messages on what to do next. You are not alone, and things are working out in your favor.

# Meet the Author

# About the Author

La'Shawn Janell: La'Shawn debuted her first collection of poetry "Evolution of a Butterfly's Truth" in 2019 and is returning with her sophomore work that encompasses the vast transformation that comes with wisdom, enlightenment and enhanced spirituality. Along with being an author and spoken word artist, La'Shawn continues to utilize all of her gifts, expanding into public speaking and conducting mental health and wellness workshops nationally and internationally. An athlete at heart, La'Shawn also provides mental health consulting for student-athletes and coaches young children in basketball.

Integrating spirituality and counseling is a major goal this author has, and she has been taking major strides in this direction, desiring to take the stigma off of combining both concepts.

La'Shawn's writing journey began at age 14, but she did not reveal her poetic gifts until age 20 at her alma mater, University of Delaware at an open mic event. 2007 accelerated her opportunities, encouraged to perform her pieces more consistently in Philadelphia, PA at venues such as the Arts Garage, Warmdaddy's, A Poet's Art Gallery and many other local venues in Delaware and New Jersey as well. She has worked with several musicians who have requested her collaboration to their live shows. La'Shawn has evolved into creating 'mash-ups' where she combines poetry and singing, creating a unique, intimate vibe.

Along with performing these personal pieces, La'Shawn has also hosted her own open mic events. Previously she was part of the Open Words poet collective who held monthly open mic events in PA and NJ. Her writings tend to be personal but encompass a relatability that all can connect to and with "Sage for the Wounded Soul" she is speaking to the reader about ways to heal and rise above relatable challenges. Her works continue to contain universal life themes that often boil down to our undeniable search for Love, Freedom and Belonging.

# About the Title

Since the world can be place that deals out difficult hands, I am aware that some of us feel more beaten up than others. Life can feel like a series of challenges that arise the moment you thought you were finally able to take a deep breath. If our dark valleys and wounds were visible to others, displaying on our skin as evidence that we need grace and kindness, we would all fair better day by day. However, I know that's not how life works. There are wounded souls out here that are digging down deep, mustering up the bravery to show up daily, despite the internal battles not many see. This, is for you – and me.

With this verbal sage I am spreading on these pages, I wish to pull out the discomfort so that we can look it in its eye and declare 'You cannot have me'. These wounds are not meant to be handcuffs; they are events in your rearview mirror as you have your windshield in front of you, showing you where you are going and meant to me. In order to walk freely, we must place the impact of the wounds in a box we don't step over daily. We need to rearrange the contents gently, store them away and walk lighter, only carrying the lessons and nothing else. 'Sage for the Wounded Soul' is a proclamation that though we have taken several hits, we can emerge renewed, purified and soothed; encouraged to take our power back and fly. I am rooting for you.

# Acknowledgments

**My parents:** The village and support is strong. From the first book until now, I have felt your intense pride in abundant levels. You know who you ALL are and I am blessed to have a blended family that truly cares. Mom and Dad, thank you for allowing me to soar and go after anything I have desired. I have learned determination, tenacity, ambition and sensitivity from you both. Thank you for promoting education while instilling in me that mediocrity does not exist. This has taken me further that I could imagine. Oh and that 'take no mess' attitude that courses through my veins – I know

that is from yall . I continue to be bolstered by all of your love and bravery in challenging situations. I stand tall on your shoulders and reach beyond dimensions I did not know were possible.

**My son, CJD:** Watching you grow into your own is a constant and consistent gift. You do things for me that are beyond words, Son, but just know that you inspire me daily. Your intuitive, perceptive nature is no surprise and I am excited to continue witnessing your own evolution. Your smile and laugh push me through the most taxing of days; you just being you is good enough. Your light shall not be dimmed by anyone or anything for you a divinely protected. Continue to search my eyes and find yourself in them. Thank you for being here and choosing mc.

**Vilas Pagan-Afanador:** I can feel your presence so strongly; thank you for continuing to guide me from your realm. By now you would have written three more books, and my only regret is that the world did not get more of you. I am deeply honored to have been chosen to be a lasting part of your legacy and memory. You encouraged me to write the first book, and I can say it is slightly bittersweet to be completing a second without you here physically. I know you're around though, so there is no doubt your loving presence is woven throughout my work. I am forever thankful to you.

**My publisher Dave Jr., Ware:** We have come a long way! Planting that initial seed of becoming an author has me on a road I do not see stopping anytime soon. Thank you for believing in my gift and artistry.

**My fellow Poets/Artists:** Go Off!! None of this even crossed my own mind without the encouragement and support of some of the most creative, genius minds I have meant on this poetic journey. I am honored to be one of 'y'all'. These stages and safe spaces are a sanctuary for me where I can express and all is well. There is absolutely nothing like it. You all continue to be a source of mind-blowing inspiration for me – the world **needs** us. We are the historians and thought leaders that do not get nearly enough credit. I salute you and I thank you for being a light in this world.

**Friends and family:** I feel you even if I do not see you often. Your love radiates beyond the physical realm and I know who to call when I need to get out of this creative mind and be present. Thank you for rocking and rolling with me through my most tumultuous and turbulent moments that end up in poetry like this ☺. Your conversations have helped me clarify my purpose and catapulted me into persevering even when the days are rough. There are not even words to express my overflowing gratitude for your presence.

# WARERESOURCES AND PUBLISHING

# WE ARE AN ALL IN ONE,

# ONE STOP PUBLISHING COMPANY!!!!

W.R.P. is a modest but skillful and knowledgeable Christian Publishing Company. We specialize in getting authors into print. We embrace and guide each author like a member of our family. We treat you fairly and recognize the importance of building a lasting relationship with you as an author. Join us in the walk to promote prosperity along with the message of encouragement and peace. Be one of the authors we transform and prepare for the world of information and books.

FEEL FREE TO CONTACT US@

www.wareresources.com

1-800-469-4850 EXT. 2

Facebook: Book Publisher Dave Jr., Ware

Printed in the USA
CPSIA information can be obtained
at www.ICGtesting.com
CBHW050436301024
16597CB00012B/134